A Poetry Collection

Muted Damages

Poems from a Black Sheep's Hidden Struggles with Family Emotional Abuse, Self-Discovery, and Quiet Resilience

Drew Mackby Sand

Muted Damages © by *Drew Mackby Sand 2024.*

All rights reserved. No part of this book may be reproduced, stored in a retrieval system, or transmitted in any form or by any means, electronic or mechanical, without the prior written permission of the publisher. Exceptions are made for brief quotations in critical reviews or articles. This book is intended for informational purposes only and is not a substitute for professional advice or treatment.

First Edition 2024
A catalogue record of this book is with the Library & Archives Canada.

Independently Published
Names: Drew Mackby Sand
Title: Muted Damages
Identifiers: ISBN 978-1-0690582-0-1

Contents

Introduction 7

Echoes of a Black Sheep 9
- Exploring the experience of feeling different, isolated, and misunderstood within the family and community. Reflects on the emotional impact of defying expectations and struggle of individuality.

Beneath the Family Tree 31
- Delving into family dynamics and the pain of strained or severed relationships. Unveils the wounds of betrayal and toxicity, revealing the emotional scars left by a troubled upbringing.

To My Younger Self 139
- Letters of reflection, advice, and compassion directed towards my younger self. A dialogue with the past, offering wisdom and care that were once missing.

Becoming 171
- Capturing the journey of self-discovery, healing, and resilience. Poems chart the path from despair to hope, celebrating moments of clarity and strength along the way.

Finding Home 207
- Celebrating the reclamation of identity and embracing uniqueness. Reflects on breaking free from family expectations and discovering a self-defined sense of belonging and personal acceptance.

I just wanted to express how I feel

Introduction

Welcome to *Muted Damages,* a profound exploration of the silent struggles and quiet resilience of a black sheep navigating the stormy seas of family emotional trauma. This collection of poems is a deeply personal journey through the pain and isolation experienced when one feels like an outcast not only within their family but also within their community.

In these pages, you will find raw and evocative reflections on surviving a toxic, dysfunctional household—where emotional wounds are inflicted in silence, and the scars often remain hidden. The poems capture the profound loneliness of being misunderstood and marginalized, offering an unflinching look at the impact of growing up in an environment where one's individuality and needs are overshadowed by dysfunction.

Muted Damages unfolds in stages, beginning with the stark reality of being the black sheep, an outsider whose very existence challenges family norms. Each poem in this collection is a window into the experience of rejection and the quest for validation amid emotional abuse. Through vivid language and poignant imagery, I lay bare the struggles of feeling unseen and unheard, giving voice to the silent suffering that often goes unacknowledged.

Muted Damages

As you journey through these poems, you will witness the transition from isolation to liberation. This collection charts the arduous path from grappling with deep-seated pain to discovering self-worth and building resilience. It is a testament to the courage required to face one's demons, reclaim one's identity, and find freedom on one's own terms.

Ultimately, *Muted Damages* is a celebration of the strength found in vulnerability and the power of self-acceptance. It offers solace and understanding to those who have felt alone in their struggles and serves as a reminder that even in the quietest of battles, there is hope and a path to healing. I invite you to read with an open heart and to find echoes of your own journey within these pages.

Echoes of a Black Sheep

Poems exploring the experience of being different, isolated, or misunderstood within family or community. This section delves into the identity of the black sheep, reflecting on the emotional reverberations of defying expectations and embracing individuality.

Born Different

In the mirror's reflection,
I see a face that stands alone—
Different, not by choice, but by birth,
A black sheep in a sea of conformity.

Sometimes, pride swells within me,
For not following the herd,
For thinking outside the prescribed lines,
For daring to be a different shade.

Yet, with pride comes a shadow,
A twinge of shame I can't shake,
For the very traits I cherish
Are the ones that set me apart.

In solitude, I embrace my unique path,
The dreams that flicker far from the norm,
But envy and regret whisper too,
Longing for a place in the crowd I never fit.

I sway between these polar tides—
Pride in my distinct light,
And sorrow for the solitude it brings,
Forever caught between joy and lament.

Out of Place

In this town, I stand apart,
A difference they can't ignore.
I'm not what they expect,
A misfit in their narrow view.

Their eyes hold silent judgment,
Their whispers sting with scorn.
I walk my own path,
While they follow a single road.

Their rules press down heavy,
Conformity is their only goal.
Here I remain,
An outsider in their world,
Longing for acceptance I'll never find.

The Unseen Tree

In a forest of conformity,
Where every tree stands straight and still,
I am a wild, twisted sapling,
Mocked for my defiance,
Scorned for reaching in directions unknown.

Their whispers are a chorus of judgment,
Voices that lash out at my uneven limbs,
They shape their branches to fit the norm,
While I am battered by their cruel wind,
My growth a target for their disdain.

Roots that wind through the soil in protest
Are condemned as flaws, my struggle
A subject of ridicule, their laughter
Echoing through the forest's unforgiving expanse,
Where my attempts to be myself are met with scorn.

In their eyes, I am the tree that defies,
Bearing fruit that sours their perfect yield,
Each attempt to grow beyond their sight
Invites harsh words and unkind blows,
Their mockery a chain to bind my spirit.

Their hands, poised to prune the oddities,
Banish my branches to the shadows,
Where the coldness of their judgment

Echoes of a Black Sheep

Is a constant frost, stifling the wild
That seeks to burst forth in me.

The forest floor is strewn with fallen leaves
Of those who dared to be different,
Their voices silenced by the weight
Of a relentless norm that demands compliance,
Or suffers the wrath of its harsh enforcers.

I reach for the light that dares to peek through,
A pale beam in a sky of unyielding gray,
Fighting the constant barrage of mockery
And the icy chill of their contempt,
Seeking to find a place where I am accepted.

But the winds of change are laced with venom,
A cold, biting gust that lashes at my bark,
Reminding me of the pain endured
When my roots refused to conform,
And my leaves were not what they wanted.

Still, I stand as a testament to defiance,
Despite their attempts to bend me to their will,
A wild tree in a forest that never sees,
My growth a testament to enduring
The storms of their harsh, unforgiving gaze.

Chained by Approval

I constantly chase the phantom of approval,
Bending myself to fit their vision,
Struggling to be seen, to be valued,
Yet feeling more isolated with every attempt,
Caught in a loop of unfulfilled demands.

The shame of not meeting their standards,
Of being a constant disappointment,
Crushes my spirit, dims my light,
As I try to find my place in a world
That refuses to see me as I am.

Compromised Self

The burden of expectations weighs heavy,
A relentless demand to blend in,
Each smile a façade, each nod a surrender,
To the roles they impose, the paths they lay.
My own dreams are ghosts in the background.

Desperation to be accepted
Turns me into a shadow of myself,
People-pleasing becomes a survival tactic,
While the essence of who I am
Fades into the fringes of their reality.

Molded into Silence

I am a shape not of my own making,
Pressed into molds that never fit,
Straining to align with the expectations,
Of a world that only sees me
In the narrow lines they've drawn.

Every day is a careful balancing act,
Wearing masks to blend in,
My own voice a whisper drowned out
By the cacophony of demands,
Each step a dance to a rhythm that isn't mine.

Echoes of Unbelonging

In this world where conformity reigns,
I've been taught to shrink and bend,
To suppress the flickers of who I am,
Until I am but a ghost in their shadow,
An outsider to my own existence.

The pressure to fit into their mold,
To meet expectations I never set,
Leaves me hollow, a mere reflection
Of their desires, while my own truth
Remains locked away, unseen.

Echoes of a Black Sheep

Forced Alignment

In the corners of this small town,
Where each face is a mirror
Of conformity, I have learned
To wear masks, to shape my edges
To fit the narrow lines drawn
By family's tight embrace,
By the expectations carved
Into the daily grind.

I am not made for the molds,
Yet I squeeze myself into them,
A people pleaser by necessity,
Each smile a veneer,
Each gesture a rehearsed act,
Hoping to blend into the sea
Of familiar, unchanging faces.

But every step feels like sand
Through an hourglass, slipping,
An outsider in my own skin,
Struggling to follow paths
That never aligned with my compass.

The weight of their eyes,
The judgment in their silence,
Shame wraps around me like chains,
Crippling, suppressive, unyielding.

Echoes of a Black Sheep

I yearn to escape these bindings,
To be seen without pretense,
But in this small town, and this family,
My true self remains a ghost,
Haunting the edges of conformity.

Unseen Self

I grew up in a world that demands conformity,
Where stepping out of line means isolation,
And being different is a crime.
I learned early on that to fit in,
I must lose myself, become someone else,
A reflection of their expectations, not mine.

In family gatherings, in the streets,
I played the role, wore the mask,
Smiled when I felt hollow,
Agreed when my heart screamed otherwise,
All to avoid the sting of rejection,
The crippling shame of being out of step.

The people-pleasing became second nature,
A shield against their judgments,
A way to blend into the background,
To avoid the pain of standing alone,
Yet every smile felt like a betrayal,
Every gesture a compromise of my true self.

Now I am a ghost in my own life,
Haunted by the expectations I never embraced,
Desperately wanting to be seen,
But feeling trapped in a script
That never fit my soul's desires.

Halloween's Refuge

In a place where I felt like an outsider,
shame and trauma were my constant companions.
Family traditions came with strings,
guilt and control tied to every gesture,
my worth measured by their demands.

Birthdays and Christmas were battles,
each gift a weight, each favor a chain.
Their love was conditional,
a currency I could never repay,
my spirit chafed under the strain.

But Halloween was different.
On this night, the masks were mine to choose,
not to hide, but to be.
Costumes offered freedom,
an escape from the roles I was forced to play.

No expectations, no obligations—
just the thrill of the strange and unusual,
a space where my love for the odd
was met with acceptance, not scorn.
Halloween was my reprieve,
a brief moment of relief from the pressures
that always weighed heavy on my heart.

Echoes of a Black Sheep

Silenced Truths

As a child,
you are told what to believe—
obedience is goodness.
Speaking your truth is talking back,
disrespectful, rude,
anger met with punishment.

You're not overwhelmed, they say,
just shy.
Your feelings don't matter
like theirs do.
Their needs, their joy,
always first.
Even when it means your humiliation,
your shame.

Use your head, not your heart—
intuition is just a trick.
Since birth, I was taught
to deny what I knew,
by those who convinced me
they knew better.

Between Two Worlds

As I grew older, the difference became clear:
an outsider in my own home, my community,
my family felt foreign,
strange in their shadows.

I longed for a sibling as a friend,
not a rival who bullied,
and parents who would accept me,
support my dreams,
even if I seemed different.

When I moved away and stood alone,
I found friends who listened,
allowing me to be myself,
free from pretense.

Back home, my words were ignored,
misunderstood and twisted,
leaving me feeling unworthy,
lost among strangers.

I once thought the fault was mine,
but learned it was their perception.
Now I stand firm in my truth,
yet the bitterness of betrayal lingers,
the sting of rejection remains,
echoing shadows from the past.

Echoes of a Black Sheep

Scars of a Black Sheep

Slowly, silently, I am dying,
Worn down by family, crushed by life,
My spirit bruised, my truth ignored,
Each time I speak, my words dismissed,
Or twisted into bitter fights,
So now I keep my silence close,
Heart aching for someone to hear,
To see the wounds that never show,
The scars that linger on my soul.

Those who say they care the most,
Do not know me, never will,
Surrounded by the narcissists,
By bullies who pretend to love,
Who've never seen the real me,
The one who aches to break the mold,
But every time I try to speak,
My voice is met with sharp disdain.

Born into a town of walls,
The black sheep lost in hostile fields,
Authenticity suppressed,
Each truth I shared was met with spite,
My spirit shattered, heart undone,
I seek the quiet trees instead,
For they know me better than those
Who've watched me grow, yet never cared.

Echoes of a Black Sheep

I crave the safety of alone,
Where no one speaks and no one harms,
For solitude is where I find
The peace denied in all my years—
I am the black sheep, born to roam,
Yearning just to be seen whole,
To find a space where I am free,
Where all the broken heal in light.

Conditional Love

The greatest betrayal,
a heartbreak deeper than any,
is realizing since birth
I've been taught to deny myself
by those who claim to care.

But it was never about love—
only their comfort.
Unless I fit their mold,
a reflection of their own image,
I am unworthy
of approval,
of love,
of support.

Quiet Corners

There's a quiet joy
In building a world
Of your own
Where others can't intrude.

I gather essentials,
Things to sustain me
In the corners of space
I can call my own.

And in these quiet corners,
I am whole
Without needing
Their approval.

The Black Sheep's Path

It's the black sheep
who are set to lead
into a new world.
The outcasts,
the outsiders,
the ones who never fit
with societal norms.

We felt the world's rejection,
so we carved out spaces
where we could exist
without fitting in.
We learned to be okay
with not belonging,
to find peace
in our own way.

Now, others are waking up,
seeing that what once worked
no longer fits.
They turn to the paths
we've blazed,
embracing what we discovered:
living harmoniously with nature,
rejecting the corporate control
that once ruled us.

Echoes of a Black Sheep

We're moving toward a slower pace,
a life of independence,
finding peace in simplicity.
In this new way of being,
we find our place,
redefining what it means
to belong.

The black sheep's journey
is not just survival;
it's a path to something greater,
to a world where our differences
are not just accepted
but celebrated.

Beneath the Family Tree

An exploration of family dynamics and the complexities that shape us. This section reveals the pain of strained or severed relationships, highlighting betrayal, hurt, and the realization of toxicity. Through raw honesty, these poems uncover the roots of my upbringing and the emotional scars left behind.

Beneath the Family Tree

The Weight of Expectations

In the fragile space between them,
my worth is measured by their dreams,
a currency spent on fulfilling
the aspirations that never belonged to me.

Their expectations are a scaffold,
built on the shifting sands of their desires,
each beam and nail a testament
to the pressure I feel to conform.

I am asked to blend, to mold
my essence into the shapes they desire,
leaving fragments of myself behind
to satisfy their unmet goals.

Each critique is a thread,
woven into the fabric of my self-doubt,
a tapestry of what I am not,
where my individuality is lost
in the shadow of their ambitions.

Beneath the Family Tree

The Chisel and the Stone

Their aspirations are chisels,
carving away at the stone of who I am,
each chip a demand for conformity,
a relentless pursuit of their vision.

I am sculpted into a form
that fits their expectations,
my uniqueness reduced to dust
as they mold me into their ideal.

Their criticism is the hammer,
pounding away at my self-worth,
shaping me into a reflection of their desires,
while my own qualities fade beneath the force.

The Silent Echo

Their voices are echoes,
repeating the same demands,
a chorus of expectations that drowns
the whispers of my true self.

In their presence, I am silenced,
my individuality a casualty
to their relentless push for conformity,
a sacrifice to the altar of their dreams.

Each criticism is a note,
striking a chord of worthlessness
that reverberates through my being,
leaving me to search for echoes of myself
in the quiet spaces they leave behind.

Beneath the Family Tree

The Cost of Validation

Every conversation is a battleground,
where logic is twisted and truth obscured,
not for clarity, but for the pleasure
of inflating their hollow selves.

Their egos are fragile, spun from fear,
demanding affirmation through derision,
a cruel exchange where my worth
is sacrificed on the altar of their validation.

Their need for superiority
is a cage, locking me away
from the freedom to be myself,
forcing silence as my only escape.

I have learned that peace lies
beyond their reach, in the calm of separation,
where I am free from the need to defend
against their ceaseless need to control.

Beneath the Family Tree

Mother

To those outside,
she's all smiles and kindness—
an angel in disguise,
always ready to lend a hand
or play the caring friend.
But behind the scenes,
she's a master of manipulation,
a puppeteer who tugs at strings
no one else can see.

To her children,
she's a relentless force,
covertly narcissistic,
turning every interaction
into a power struggle.
She twists the truth,
bends reality to fit her needs,
wearing a mask of innocence
while pulling us down
with her relentless grip.

Her charm is a facade—
a tool to deceive,
to keep her hands clean
while controlling every step we take.
She demands gratitude,
obedience masked as love,

Beneath the Family Tree

and the moment you resist,
she's the victim,
and you're the ungrateful child.
It's a trap that looks like care
but feels like chains,
where boundaries are just lines
for her to cross
without a second thought.

The Unbearable Weight

The facade of benevolence
is just that—
a facade,
to soothe their own insecurities.
They need to be seen as good,
as valuable,
while we are just pawns
in their game of self-aggrandizement.

The space we gain
is a fragile peace,
fleeting and superficial.
The true cost is the erosion of self,
the constant reminder
of their dominance,
of their power disguised
as family care.

I am trapped in this dynamic,
chained to their expectations
and my own despair.
If change does not come soon,
the weight of this existence
will be too much to bear.

The Manipulation

The children are a tool,
a means to an end,
not for love but for ego.
Parents bask in the illusion of grandeur,
their self-importance fueled
by the presence of youth.

We barter with our time,
a respite from demands,
to escape the ceaseless noise
and the weight of daily burdens.
In return, they gain their sense of worth,
relishing their role as cherished grandparents,
though their actions are marred by control
and emotional abuse.

This is not a family dynamic
but a power play,
a toxic entanglement
where love is conditional
and self-worth is manufactured.
I am suffocating in this environment,
a prisoner to their needs
and my own disillusionment.

Beneath the Family Tree

The Chains of Celebration

In festive lights and holiday cheer,
Tradition stands, unyielding, clear.
To others, it's a time of joy,
To me, it's where control destroys.

Christmas, birthdays, and those days
When cheer masks unspoken ways,
My father's gifts, a chain of worth,
And my mother's needs, a tool for mirth.

Tradition's role, a constant test,
To keep control and feel impressed.
Her need for power, his for pride,
Made holidays a place to hide.

Gifts meant to show a heart's embrace,
Were tied to worth, to set the pace.
A price was paid in guilt and dread,
Where joy was lost and tears were shed.

I wished for moments free of strain,
Where memories were not in vain.
Instead, the season's true demand
Was bound by rules of her command.

In each tradition's rigid frame,
There lay a plot to stake a claim.

Beneath the Family Tree

For every gift, each holiday's scene,
Was a tool to keep me unseen.

So, while others seek joy's light,
I grapple with these chains each night,
Desiring a break from guilt and pain,
Where holidays are not in vain.

Beneath the Family Tree

Behind the Facade

Only after I left home
did I see what family could be—
warmth and health, a world apart
from the cold discord I'd known.

I tried to mend what was broken,
burdened with the weight of change,
only to find I was chasing shadows,
grasping at a façade I could never truly unveil.

How do you explain a toxic home
to those who see only a polished mask,
when the truth hides in the cracks
they've never had to see?

Echoes of Unspoken Affection

Affection was absent in our home—
"I love you" was a phrase my parents never used.
Hugs were strangers in our lives,
Unfamiliar gestures in a landscape of silence.

Now, if they tried, their attempts would be stiff,
A painful reminder of what was never given.
Their touch and their words would seem insincere,
A distant echo of love never learned.

The Guilt of Generosity

Holidays meant to bring joy,
Were marred by strings and expectations,
Each gift a reminder of duty,
Not of unconditional love.

My father's extravagant gestures,
Tied to demands and control,
A facade of generosity,
Concealing his need to dominate.

And my mother's favors, a currency,
Used to guilt and manipulate,
Every act of kindness a bargaining chip,
Turning love into a tool for obedience.

The Cycle of Disempowerment

A cycle of control and conflict,
Where boundaries lead to arguments,
A pattern of disempowerment,
In a home where my needs were secondary.

The refusal to acknowledge my efforts,
The constant need for validation,
Left me feeling disempowered,
In a system where my voice was stifled.

Even as I tried to help,
Every action became a battleground,
A struggle to balance my well-being
With the demands of a toxic environment.

So I chose to step back,
To protect my own peace,
Leaving behind the futile battles,
For the sake of my emotional health.

Beneath the Family Tree

Boundaries and Conflict

Establishing boundaries with toxic family,
A task that feels insurmountable,
Brings conflict and contention,
A struggle to put my own needs first.

Raised in fear of confrontation,
Where authority ruled without question,
My efforts to set limits were met with resistance,
Every line drawn sparked a battle.

Distance became my safeguard,
To protect my peace and well-being,
When every boundary I set
Only fueled further conflict.

My needs were deemed insignificant,
In a house where rules were unbending,
Where authority claimed ownership
Over people and shared spaces.

In trying to offer help, I faced opposition,
My intentions misunderstood,
A mother's need for control
Stifled any attempt at independence.

The battle for space and voice,
A constant clash of wills,

Eventually led to withdrawal,
To preserve my sanity and avoid further strife.

Beneath the Family Tree

The Price of Help

Offering to cook, a gesture of goodwill,
Met with scorn and dismissal,
A mother's disdain for shared tasks,
Her need for control masked as preference.

My efforts to ease her burden
Rejected with excuses and complaints,
Even a beloved dish met with resistance,
An attempt at help turned to a point of contention.

The structure imposed on shared spaces,
A rigid control that stifled independence,
Her need to be needed, a driving force,
That left no room for family contributions.

Conflict arose with every step I took,
Trying to contribute, to be of use,
Yet the constant pushback and resistance
Made it clear, peace required retreat.

Her need for control overshadowed
any willingness to accept support.
In shunning my attempts,
she reinforced her own sense of importance,
making me dependent
to feed her need for self-worth.

Invisible Wounds

In the shadow of emotional abuse,
a spirit withers, unseen.
A silent cry echoes in a toxic space
where only the victim senses the pain.

Enduring torment that remains invisible,
living with poison masked as care,
while the world stays oblivious
to the chains that confine,
and the wounds that bleed in quiet despair.

Tasks demanded, belittled if unmet,
labeled as ignorant for deviations or questions.
Every action is scrutinized, every move criticized,
with no room for independence.

They are reminded they are not a child but an employee,
subject to micromanagement,
taught to depend and be respectful,
in silence and obedience,
seeking worth and approval
under an oppressive rule,
yet it was never given.

This is the story of a broken soul,
resilient yet invisible and unheard,
carrying the burden of unseen scars.

Beneath the Family Tree

The Curse of Unseen Reflections

I used to joke that my parents were cursed,
but now, as I understand energy,
I see a truth in that jest.

While working for my father,
my mental health plummeted.
I saw a side of him
that favored some employees
over others, creating discord
and tension among the staff.

I watched him pit people
against each other, ignore ideas
that weren't his, belittle those
trying to contribute positively.
He often joked about being an asshole,
but it wasn't until I worked for him
that I saw how he truly treated people—
disrespectfully, with lost temper,
pissing off many.

When anger and hatred are directed
toward you, they manifest as
negative occurrences. Disrespect
toward others brings karma,
a cycle of hate and malice.

Beneath the Family Tree

My parents refuse to see
that their treatment of others
is the source of their own mistreatment.
They continue to play victims,
deny responsibility, and refuse
to acknowledge their role
in their own misfortunes.

They cannot admit mistakes,
cannot say "I'm sorry,"
because it would require
reflection and emotional growth.
They, and my sister,
are emotionally stunted,
incapable of seeing themselves
as the root of their problems.

The Limits of Understanding

There is a reason for the distance
between us, a reason
I no longer want a relationship
with her.

We have had countless conversations
about accountability, about boundaries,
and yet she continues
to disregard both.

The emotional abuse inflicted on us,
from childhood into adulthood,
remains unacknowledged.
She refuses to accept responsibility,
convinced she is blameless.

What my sister and I have endured
with manipulation and abuse
is beyond the comprehension
of those not in our shoes.

Unless you've lived it,
you cannot see
the emotional abuse masked
by her outward charm.

Her denial is a fortress,
one she will never dismantle.

Beneath the Family Tree

To her, her needs are paramount,
her image, a façade of greatness.

As children, we were shaped
to please her, to inflate her ego,
while our own self-worth dwindled
to nothing.

Despite our attempts
to heal, to communicate,
she reverts to her toxic ways,
showing no interest in change.

Her concern lies with her image,
not with the pain she causes.
To those on the outside,
it remains unseen,
for it is not overt,
but subtle and insidious.

Living with her has been a trial,
a lesson in enduring toxicity
despite knowing the strategies
to set boundaries and protect myself.

I am weary of defending
my choices to those
who have not lived our reality.
I need distance to safeguard
my peace and well-being.

Beneath the Family Tree

Explaining the Unseen

Explaining it to you
isn't easy.
You don't see the strings she pulls,
the way she twists things
until she's the victim
and I'm the one to blame.
But you've been caught in her web,
just like I was,
and you don't even know it.

It's crucial you understand—
this isn't just about her and me.
She's manipulated you, too,
made you believe her stories,
her lies.
You've become her enablers,
unwittingly giving her the power
to continue the cycle.

I need you to see
that healing from her abuse
isn't a simple path.
It's painful,
complicated,
and requires more than just time.
I have to protect myself,
create distance,

Beneath the Family Tree

set boundaries
that can't be crossed.

When my boundaries are violated,
there are consequences,
and yes,
that might mean less contact—
with her,
with you.

It's not that I don't want family,
but being close means
being constantly triggered,
pulled back into a cycle
I'm trying to escape.

I know you might not see it,
might not understand,
but I need you to try.
She's not what she seems,
and her influence
has stretched beyond me.
Until you see that,
support within this family
is something I can't find.

Under Her Thumb

Growing up,
I was always under her thumb,
dependent, suppressed,
like a puppet she kept close
to feed her need for control.

Every decision,
every move,
she made for me—
not because she cared,
but because she needed me needy.
My reliance fed her,
validated her,
made her feel important.

She couldn't stand the thought
of me standing tall,
of me outshining her.
So, she kept me small,
discouraged my achievements,
projected her insecurities
onto me,
until I began to believe
they were mine.

To the outside world,
she was the devoted mother,

Beneath the Family Tree

loving, caring.
But inside our home,
it was different.
Her fragile image needed protecting,
and I was the shield.
Guilt and fear
became her tools,
keeping me in line,
keeping me compliant.

Who I was
didn't matter—
my identity,
overshadowed by her need
to feel indispensable.

Now, I see it.
The manipulation,
the control,
the way she stunted my growth.
I struggle now—
low self-esteem,
blurred boundaries,
the challenge of forming
healthy relationships.

But knowing this,
this awareness,
is a step.

Beneath the Family Tree

A step toward healing,
a step toward breaking the cycle,
toward a healthier way
to be.

The Price of Love

You think she means well.
You believe her stories.
But did you ever wonder
why I flinch at the sound of her name?

Why I keep my distance,
even when you call it unnecessary?

Her love comes with conditions,
her care with a price.
And I cannot pay anymore.

Beneath the Family Tree

Self-Serving

It's clear as day—
Dad's advice,
his words dressed as wisdom,
are for him alone.
Every suggestion,
each plan he lays before me,
is rooted in what he wants,
not what I need.

He frames it with careful pauses,
reverse psychology at play,
making it seem like my idea,
while pulling strings I can't see.
His interest isn't mine,
it never was.
Every choice,
every push,
is to serve himself,
wrapped in the guise of fatherly concern.

He will never give without taking,
never speak without calculation.
His needs come first,
and always will.

A self-serving bastard,
through and through,

Beneath the Family Tree

hiding behind the mask
of care,
but never lifting a hand
unless it feeds his own desire.

Plain and simple,
he'll never put me first.
His heart beats for no one
but himself.

Tethered

She taught me dependence,
tethered me to her needs.
Made sure I'd never fly too far,
lest she lose her grip
on the version of me she'd crafted.

Her approval dangled,
always out of reach,
and my self-worth,
always measured against her shifting standards.

Defending a Lie

They defend her,
because they have only ever known her smile,
not the sneer she hides so well.
They didn't see her raise her voice in silence,
or feel the coldness that followed
whenever I stepped out of line.

I've tried to speak,
but they've grown deaf to anything
that disrupts their picture of her.
To them,
she is warmth.
To me,
she is ice.

The Stage She Owns

She whispers the loudest when no one listens.
Her kindness is a show,
a spectacle for others to admire.

But I know the stage lights go dark
when the doors close,
and the script she reads from
is one she wrote to keep me small.

Silent Strings

They don't see it,
how her words twist softly,
how her hands guide without pressure—
just a constant pull.
She speaks of love,
yet plants doubt in every sentence.

They think she means well,
but I live beneath her shadow.
Her needs always above my own.
They stand on the outside,
believing her stories,
never hearing the silence between her lies.

Beneath the Family Tree

Trapped in a Cycle

The days blend into one,
each marked by the same question:
When?
When will I break free
from the grip of control
and start living my own life?

The work I've put in
feels overshadowed
by the lack of progress,
my motivation slipping away
like sand through fingers.

In this toxic space,
each effort feels futile,
as if I'm working against
an unrelenting force
that keeps me anchored
in this place I loathe.

I've found some enjoyment
in what I do,
yet the joy is marred
by the endless frustration
of being surrounded
by negativity and judgment.

Beneath the Family Tree

The dream of escape
seems increasingly distant,
clouded by financial constraints
and the harsh reality
of a world that feels
both oppressive and indifferent.

My spirit feels battered,
crushed under the weight
of familial control
and societal failures.
I long for a sanctuary,
a place of peace and solitude
where I can reclaim
a semblance of hope.

But finding that peace
seems like an impossible task,
as every attempt
to move forward
feels like navigating
through a blizzard of obstacles.

I question whether
I've done enough,
if my efforts are sufficient
or if the world
is simply set against me.

Escape from Delusion

Their world is a cage,
a small, narrow space
filled with delusions
and judgments.

I see their ignorance,
their inability to understand
the truth of my life,
the reality beyond their control.

Their criticisms,
their unwelcome opinions,
are a constant barrier
to my freedom,
to my peace.

I long to escape,
to find a space
free from their delusions,
where I can live
without their shadows
looming over me.

Living Under Their Shadow

I live under their shadow,
their opinions like a weight
pressing down,
a constant reminder
of their small-mindedness.

Their judgments are unasked,
unwanted,
shaping every interaction
into a battlefield
of delusion and control.

I stay silent,
not out of agreement,
but to avoid the barrage
of their criticisms,
their unwillingness
to see beyond their own narrow view.

The Unasked Opinions

They speak,
their words filled with judgment
and delusions,
unaware of the truth.

Their unsolicited opinions
cut through the air,
harsh and unwanted,
as if they know better.

I've stopped explaining,
stopped sharing,
because their reactions
are never kind.

Their world is small,
their understanding shallow.
They live in their own bubble,
dismissing the reality outside.

Delusional Conversations

Sitting at the dinner table,
I hear their voices,
a clamor of small-mindedness,
delusions wrapped in certainty.

Mom brings up something,
a topic turned into a judgment,
a misunderstanding
wrapped in accusations.

"You're withholding information,"
she says,
as if I owe them details
of my life's every step.

The truth is simpler—
I keep my plans to myself
to avoid their unsolicited opinions,
their shaming gaze.

Their control is exhausting,
their judgments intrusive.
I'd rather be silent
than subject myself to their delusions.

Losing Hope

I don't know what to do anymore.
I've tried everything,
but nothing changes.

I feel like I'm drowning
in this toxic environment,
losing hope,
losing patience,
losing myself.

I've asked for guidance,
but all I get is silence.
I'm tired,
so fucking tired.
All I want is to live
my own life,
but it feels like I'm stuck
in this endless cycle
of waiting.

Trapped

I feel trapped—
in this house,
in this family,
in this cycle of misery.

I've been trying to escape
since I can remember,
trying to figure out
how to support myself,
how to be independent.
But every step I take
feels like I'm walking in quicksand,
sinking deeper
into this toxic place.

I just want to get out,
to start over,
but it feels impossible.

Personal Hell

This place is my personal hell,
no space to think,
no freedom to breathe.
I've tried the spiritual—
visualizing, praying, manifesting,
and the practical—
as much action as I could muster.

Nothing works.
The universe keeps asking me
to be patient,
but I can't.
I'm done with waiting,
done with hoping
for a way out.

I just want to live
my own life,
to be independent,
to escape the control
that wraps around me
like a chokehold.

Inheritance

Your control drips slowly
into their minds,
a quiet poison
they don't know they swallow.
I watch it shape them,
bend them,
until the lines between
you and them
blur.

They don't see the bars,
don't know the prison
they've inherited.
But I do.
And the weight of that knowing
is a burden
I can no longer carry.

Under Her Watch

I can't reach them
without reaching through her,
my every move weighed
in her hands,
permission always the price
to see their faces.

She stands there,
a silent gatekeeper,
her eyes watching
every word,
every smile,
turning moments into something
I can hardly bear.

She knows what she's doing—
how each visit,
each time spent together
is chipped away,
until all that's left
is the cold distance
she's carved between us.

It's unbearable,
the way her shadow falls
over everything,
her presence too loud

Beneath the Family Tree

even in silence.
She keeps them close,
not out of love,
but out of power.

She knows I would teach them
to stand on their own,
to see the world
without her hands
on their shoulders.
But she won't allow it—
she tightens her grip
every time I reach out,
making sure I never get
a moment alone.

She's destroying what could be,
what should be,
so they stay hers,
forever reliant
on the control
she calls love.

Permission to Breathe

It's exhausting,
the way every move
is measured, weighed,
passed through her hands
like a gatekeeper
of moments I never get
to hold alone.

A smile twisted by permission.
A laugh cut short by control.
Her grip is invisible,
but I feel it everywhere.

The Contract

Time with them
is a contract
I never signed.
Every moment feels rented,
a loan with conditions
I didn't agree to.
You keep taking more
until there's nothing left
worth keeping.

Done

I'm tired of asking permission
to love.

Impatient

I am so impatient.
Done with this phase,
done with the old me,
buried in the past.
I'm ready to live freely,
to break from this prison
of control and manipulation,
to step out of the shadows
of my mother's grip.

Her judgment, her shame,
it's too much—
too heavy to carry.
I see it now.
I need to leave,
to breathe without her
watching my every move.

I can't stand this house,
this family,
this toxic place
where I have no space,
no freedom.
I'm ready for a new beginning,
a life that's mine.

The Echoes of Discontent

In the cacophony of family conflict,
words are weapons,
apologies empty shells,
their echoes resounding
in the chambers of a wounded heart.

The struggle is a constant
back-and-forth of unmet needs,
a cycle of discontent
draining the spirit's vigor.

Escape becomes a dream,
a whisper in the tumult,
a hope for solitude
that offers a respite
from the pervasive negativity.

The journey forward
is marked by patience,
by the quiet rebellion
of staying true
to one's authentic self.

Beneath the Family Tree

Unconditional Embrace

I envy families where love is straightforward.
Siblings and parents who genuinely accept each other,
sharing laughter and playfulness without reservation.
In their home, there is no space for criticism or judgment,
just a clear and unconditional embrace of who they are.

They interact with openness, without fear of shame or scorn.
Every moment is an expression of their true selves,
without the need to hide or conform.
Their relationships are marked by trust and understanding,
a sanctuary where love is expressed freely and fully.

I watch them and long for such a connection,
where acceptance and authenticity are simply given,
and every interaction is a testament to a loving, supportive bond.

Beneath the Family Tree

The Bully Father

In the house where authority should dwell,
my father reigns as a child,
his tantrums echoing louder
than any reason or maturity.

His opinion, a scepter of dominance,
demanded to be the only truth,
and my own thoughts are met
with the scorn of a king unchallenged.

In his eyes, dissent is treachery,
a rebellion against his fragile throne.
When my voice rises,
it is crushed beneath the weight
of his childish rage.

He wields belittlement like a weapon,
each dismissive sneer a blow
to my sense of self,
each harsh word a reminder
that my worth is measured by his approval.

When my views diverge from his own,
he casts me out, a heretic
in the kingdom of his ego,
where my individuality is sacrificed
on the altar of his unyielding pride.

Beneath the Family Tree

In the shadow of his dominance,
I have learned to navigate
with a silence that protects,
a shield against the storms
of his inflated self-importance.

Here, in this distance,
I reclaim my voice,
finding strength in the quiet
that separates me from his tyranny.

Beneath the Family Tree

The Weight of Expectation

In a house where worth is measured
by conformity to another's dreams,
I am left adrift, my identity
a casualty of unmet aspirations.

My individuality is a point of contention,
a spark that ignites their insecurities,
transforming me into a mirror
for their fears and failures.

Their expectations are chains,
binding me to roles I never chose,
where my own desires are suffocated
by the weight of their unfulfilled wishes.

Beneath the Family Tree

The Poisoned Well

My family's love is a poisoned well,
filled with the bitter waters of criticism,
each sip a reminder of my inadequacy,
a reflection of their own broken selves.

Their interactions are a stage
for their egos to perform,
where I am cast as the scapegoat
for their unresolved anguish.

I have stepped away from the toxic mire,
choosing my own well-being
over the constant barrage of their need
to validate themselves at my expense.

In distancing myself, I find clarity,
a breath of fresh air beyond their reach,
where my self-worth is no longer
a casualty of their emotional warfare.

Beneath the Family Tree

Shadows on the Walls

I live in a house of shadows,
where my reality is a malleable thing,
shaped and reshaped
by the hands of another.
My mother, a maestro of illusion,
conducts a symphony of denial,
her world a stage
where only her script holds true.

Every time I speak,
my truth is met with cold denial,
her face a mask of practiced innocence.
My words, my experiences,
are rewritten in her narrative,
erased from existence,
as if they were never real,
just figments of my unstable mind.

She claims the stage, the spotlight,
while I am left in the dark,
a silent player in a drama
I never agreed to join.
Her lack of accountability,
her refusal to see the cracks
in her own crafted facade,
becomes a blade in my chest.

Beneath the Family Tree

Each contradiction, each protest
of my own lived truth
is met with a wall of deflection,
a facade so polished
it blinds those outside
to the wounds she inflicts.
She protects her image with precision,
leaving me and my sibling
adrift in a sea of distorted reflections.

The guardian of my childhood
has become the architect
of my self-doubt,
building towers of shame
where my emotions once found solace.
To question her is to be cast
into the depths of madness,
where my sanity is a casualty
of her need for control.

Recognition comes as a heavy weight,
a realization that the one
who should have nurtured
has instead been the harbinger
of my emotional desolation.
The rage and resentment
are fierce and raw,
a storm of pain that drowns
the echoes of a false love.

Beneath the Family Tree

In the aftermath,
I sift through the ruins
of a fractured reality,
haunted by the ghost
of a mother's betrayal,
her presence a relentless reminder
of the price paid for her illusion,
a bitter legacy of broken trust
and the scars of gaslit despair.

Narratives Collide

Her kindness, a façade,
an armor forged in deception,
shields her from the truth
I carry, heavy and sharp.
She rewrites our stories,
denies the echoes of my hurt,
replaces my memories
with her own narrative,
one where my reality
is but a figment
of my overactive mind.
In the shadows of her denial,
I am a ghost of my own life.

Beneath the Family Tree

The Mask of Her Virtue

Beneath the veneer of a saintly smile,
where the world sees only the shimmer
of her benevolent facade,
lies a tempest of manipulation,
a covert narcissist's masterpiece.

To those outside, she is the hero,
a paragon of kindness, a guiding light,
her actions shrouded in a veil
of selfless sacrifice and gentle care.
But to her children, she is a sorceress,
skilled in the dark arts of gaslighting,
her love a spell that ensnares,
turning our truths into whispers,
our realities into shadows.

She presents a world where
her needs come first,
her pain the only measure
of our own suffering. She wields her power
with a cruel finesse, infantilizing,
ensuring we remain bound
in the chains of her making,
dependent on her whims,
drenched in her need for validation.

Her hands mold our identities,

Beneath the Family Tree

shaping us into mirrors
of her own insecurities,
her self-worth derived
from our constant need,
our silent pleas for her approval.
She plays the victim with grace,
her tears a mask for her true face,
while behind closed doors,
her actions carve scars
into the fabric of our souls.

In her realm, every boundary
is a line drawn in shifting sands,
where our emotions are dismissed
as mere fabrications,
our struggles as inconveniences
to her perfectly constructed illusion.
She thrives in her duality,
the saintly exterior belying
the emotional turmoil she instigates,
her manipulations a dance
of calculated cruelty.

Her mask, flawless and polished,
shines brightly in the eyes of others,
while we, her children,
are left to navigate
the dark labyrinth of her making,
our pain a backdrop

Beneath the Family Tree

to her unending drama,
our trust shattered,
our identities warped,
by the very person
who should have been our refuge.

To the world, she is a beacon,
to us, a relentless storm,
her mastery of deception
a well-practiced art,
leaving us to grapple
with the shards of her truth,
forever entwined
in the destructive cycle
of her emotional abuse.

Resentment's Embrace

The truth I uncover
is wrapped in rage and sorrow,
a wound exposed
to the cold air of reality.
Her actions, a canvas
of emotional cruelty,
paint my trust in hues
of bitter resentment,
my respect eroded
by the relentless tide
of her denial.
To see the one meant to nurture
as the architect of my pain
is to confront the ruins
of my own shattered beliefs.

In the Shadow of Her Denial

When I speak, her gaze
turns to glass, cold and clear,
reflecting a truth
that she will never acknowledge.
Her voice, a silken thread,
weaves a tapestry of deceit,
where my pain is lost,
disregarded as fiction,
her image of kindness
a brittle mask over harsh reality.

In her world, my experiences
are echoes in a hollow room,
their resonance silenced
by her insistence on control.
She crafts her narrative,
a sculptor of my disbelief,
shaping my reality
into shadows of doubt,
where my truth is buried
under layers of her denial.

Each conversation, a battlefield,
where my words are met
with a wall of unyielding stone,
her lack of accountability
a chasm that swallows

Beneath the Family Tree

my voice, leaving me
to wander in the dark
of her self-preserving fog,
questioning the very essence
of my own reality.

Her refusal to see,
to acknowledge the hurt she inflicts,
turns me into a mirror
reflecting her fragile image,
a puppet in her emotional theater,
where my reality is a mere backdrop,
to the drama she enacts,
preserving her illusion
of care and control.

The constant gaslighting
etches scars into my soul,
each denial a knife
twisting in the wound,
reminding me that the one
meant to nurture and protect
has become the architect
of my anguish, shaping a reality
where my pain is dismissed,
and I am left to grapple
with the madness of her making.

In the end, the resentment

Beneath the Family Tree

I feel is a blazing fire,
consuming the remnants
of my trust and hope,
burning away the illusions
she so carefully crafted.
Her legacy is not one of love,
but of shattered reflections,
where I stand amidst the ashes,
reborn from the ashes of her denial.

Living Hell

This is my crucible,
a furnace of my own making,
where caring has become
a heavy yoke,
where respect is demanded
but never given,
where I am expected
to turn off my own feelings,
to accommodate the chaos,
and to live in the tension
of my empathy and my sanity.
In this relentless struggle,
I find only a hollow echo
of what I need to be whole.

The Weight of Empathy

They teach me to serve,
to defer,
to ignore the pain
their neglect inflicts.
I am raised in the shadow
of their needs,
a sacrifice in exchange
for shelter and sustenance.
To care is to be manipulated,
to feel is to be broken,
yet my nature rebels,
fights against the stream
of my own well-being.

Reflections in a House

Conversations with my parents
are lessons in futility.
Their house, a fortress
where my boundaries dissolve
into walls that care not
for my emotional landscapes.
I am a guest in my own existence,
an afterthought
in the narrative of their needs,
my pleas dismissed
as the whining of the undeserving,
too sensitive, too demanding
for a space that should be mine.

The Blame Game

They say it's always someone else,
always the world's fault.
They never wonder
why no one stays long,
why friends and family fade
like distant memories.

But I know.
I see what they can't.
The problem is in their hands,
in their hearts,
in their refusal to see
what they've become.

Beneath the Family Tree

Toxic Roots

A family tree
twisted at its core,
branches bent under the weight
of secrets and blame.

No one wants to stay,
no one wants to tend
a garden grown in poison.

And still,
they point fingers
at the ones who've left
instead of asking
why no one returns.

Mirrorless

They say the world's gone *wrong*,
everyone else to blame.
But the cracks aren't in the glass—
they're in the faces peering back.

If they only turned inward,
just once,
they might see the fractures
they've caused
in everyone around them.

I've watched them,
blind to their own poison,
spitting venom
and calling it truth.

And I—
I am happier
the farther I walk away
from their shattered reflections.

Beneath the Family Tree

No Room to Breathe

Their needs,
Heavy as shadows,
Creep into every corner
Of my life.

There is no room for me,
No peace
That doesn't come with cost.

I have asked,
I have pleaded
For a space of my own,
But they only hear
The echo of their desires.

Insecure Thieves

They take from me,
Not because they need,
But because they cannot bear
To see me whole.

Their insecurities
Twist into control,
Into selfish demands
That leave me
Broken at the edges.

Beneath the Family Tree

The Weight of Their Wants

Their desires hang heavy
In the air,
Pressing against my skin,
Pushing into the spaces
I once thought were mine.

But they don't care.
They can't see
Beyond their own hunger.
They would see me starve
If it meant feeding
Their fragile egos.

No Compromise

I offer the olive branch,
But they snap it in half,
Unwilling to bend
Or meet me halfway.

Their needs
Are the only ones that matter,
And I am left
With nothing but the fragments
Of a peace
That never existed.

Beneath the Family Tree

A Battle for Space

Every day is a battle
For an inch of space,
A moment of peace.

But they storm through,
Wielding their needs
Like weapons.

There's no room to breathe,
No room for me
In the wake
Of their demands.

Conversations Unheard

I've spoken until my voice is hoarse,
Laid out my heart
In the hopes they would see.

But they are blind,
Deaf to the words
That don't serve them.

Their selfishness
Consumes the air,
Leaves no room for compromise,
Only taking.

No Peace

Peace is a distant dream,
A whisper I chase
But never catch.

They shatter it
With every step,
Every word that puts them
At the center of the world.

I ask for space,
For silence,
But they fill the air
With their demands,
Leaving me empty.

Beneath the Family Tree

Feeding the Ego

Their egos
Are hungry beasts,
Devouring everything in sight.

There's nothing left
For me,
Nothing untouched
By their greed.

I have tried
To protect myself,
To set boundaries,
But they trample them
Without a second thought.

Beneath the Family Tree

Trampled Lines

The boundaries I set
For you, mother, father, sister,
Are just lines in the sand
For you to step over.

I try to hold firm,
But every time I speak,
It's like screaming into the wind.

You do not hear,
You do not care,
And I am left
With nothing but the tracks
Of your footsteps
Across my life.

Beneath the Family Tree

Left Questioning

Is it so rare to find kinship
where hearts beat in harmony,
where shared moments are not just obligations
but breaths of genuine connection?

What does it mean
to long for a family
where being yourself is not a sacrifice,
but a gift embraced and returned?

Timing the Quiet

I wait for the silence,
For the moments
When they aren't there.

Gather what I need,
Quick hands,
Silent feet,
Before slipping back
To my own space.

It's a game of timing,
Of knowing when
The storm will pass
And how to move
Without being seen.

The Art of Avoidance

I've learned the dance
Of slipping through cracks,
Of bending to silence
And timing my steps
So we do not collide.

Flexibility becomes survival,
A quiet shift in the wind,
As I bend,
And change,
And disappear.

The Mirror of Their Eyes

I move in ways
That won't disturb the air,
Careful to avoid
Their disapproval
Like the ground might crack open.

I'm learning
Their opinions
Do not define
What I am made of,
But still,
I tremble beneath their gaze.

Silent Agreements

Without words,
I've agreed to their terms.
My voice,
My space,
My time—
Handed over
Before I even realized
What I'd given away.

I'm learning
That no contract exists
Except the one
I've made with fear.

Beneath the Family Tree

The Fear of Being Seen

Shame sits beside me,
Whispering the things
I've always known:
Don't take up space,
Don't be too loud,
Don't say no.

I fear their disapproval
Like a shadow that stretches
Across every room,
Even the ones
Where I should feel free.

Muted

They control how loud
My thoughts are allowed to be.
My creativity folds
Like an envelope never sent.

I sit, unseen,
In the corner of their shared space,
Hands still,
Words stifled,
A creation buried
Before it's born.

Fear of Disapproval

I hand over my voice
Because I've been taught to fear
The sound of it.
I trade freedom for safety,
Silence for approval.

Every "no" I don't speak
Is a brick
In the wall I've built around myself.
And yet, the fear
Lingers at its edges.

Beneath the Family Tree

They Killed My Spirit

My spirit lies shattered, torn by the hands
of those who should have held me close.
I am left empty, stranded in shadows,
haunted by the weight of their words.
I am a stranger to love in my own skin,
as if my authenticity, my every breath,
is something to be scorned and silenced.

I see myself through their eyes,
a failure undeserving of kindness,
reduced to the scars they leave behind,
trapped in the echo of their ignorance.
I am weary of the endless games,
the twisting of truths until I doubt my own mind,
left questioning the reality of my wounds,
told my pain is a mirage of my making.

I am lost in the noise of their misunderstandings,
so profoundly alone in the presence of those
who should be my sanctuary.
The thought of escape flits through my mind
like a desperate whisper,
yet fear of the unknown pain holds me back,
keeping me tethered to a life
where I feel I don't belong.

I yearn for a world where my absence

Beneath the Family Tree

is not the only solace I crave,
where I can breathe without the burden
of their relentless shadows.
I am waiting for freedom,
for the courage to step beyond this toxic sphere,
to find a place where my heart
is not a battlefield but a garden of peace.

I am infinitely lighter in their absence,
a fragile flicker of hope when I am far from their reach,
longing for the day I can stand alone,
no longer bound by the chains of their disdain.
Until then, I carry the quiet, aching wish
to find myself beyond their grasp,
to rediscover my worth
in the quiet places they cannot touch.

Craving Space

I ask for space,
For air to breathe.
But all I get
Is her need to seethe.

Every boundary broken,
Every step retraced,
She invades without question,
Her need misplaced.

There's no room to grow,
No corner to hide,
When your life is ruled
By someone else's pride.

So I retreat,
But never quite enough—
Living with her is suffocation,
Disguised as love.

Bound in Love's Chains

Her love is not love,
But chains wrapped tight.
She binds me in gratitude,
Demanding my fight.

Her voice, always soft,
But her eyes, sharp and cruel,
Making me small,
Turning me into a fool.

She gave me life,
And in return,
She asks for all—
Respect that I must earn.

But love should not break,
It should not confine,
And in her grasp,
I've lost what is mine.

Beneath the Family Tree

The Weight of Tradition

Around the table, tradition's grip
Tightens with every bite—
Father's voice, a heavy hand
That steers the plates, the feast,
The order of our meal.

No say in what's prepared,
No freedom in the kitchen's heat,
Where mother's eyes, a silent storm,
Command with passive aggression
Each ingredient, each stir,
Yet refuse to taste what's made with care.

I offer my creations,
A plea for approval,
Only to meet cold indifference,
A wound wrapped in cold steel.
Freedom is a distant dream,
Unclaimed in this prison of tradition.

Beneath the Family Tree

Measured by Their Molds

Every decision, every idea, every move
was met with disdain or criticism
if it didn't match their expectations.

My mother made me feel incapable,
her dismissals a constant reminder of my flaws.
My father's approval never came
even if I mirrored his own image.

In their eyes, I was never enough,
my worth always tied to how well
I could obey and fit their mold,
my true self left in the shadows of their demands.

Beneath the Family Tree

Fractured Teamwork

Sister, we should weave a tapestry together,
But you demand that only your thread is gold.
In every stitch, your voice overshadows,
Ignoring the rich texture we could create.

Your vision, a mirror reflecting just yourself,
Colors blend into your exclusive scheme,
Yet in our combined effort lies the potential,
To craft a masterpiece far beyond your own dream.

Beneath the Family Tree

The Distant Echo

I call across a canyon, sister,
A voice, a plea, a simple question,
But your echoes return as taunts,
Deaf to the sincerity you don't hear.

Your words fall like pebbles,
Plunking into the void, creating ripples,
Yet no bridge forms, no path emerges,
Just the emptiness of unshared truths.

A One-Way Street

In the one-way street of her making,
No room for detours or crosswalks,
Her traffic lights blaze with finality,
Every turn is blocked by her own stance.

Voices are drowned in her cacophony,
Silent pleas swept aside by her roar,
A path paved by her own compass,
Leaving no space for another's lore.

The Cliff's Edge

A week more of her
and I might leap
from the edge,
driven by the weight
of her relentless
manipulative cries.

Her sickness, self-imposed,
her pleas, a façade,
a mask to escape
the duties she shirks.

The burden of her
false weakness
pushes me to the brink,
her deceitful dance
a precipice
I am near to falling from.

Beneath the Family Tree

The Burden of Care

A mother who chooses
to remain incapacitated,
consuming what harms her,
avoiding the duties
she's created.

Her state is a product
of neglect and denial,
her sickness a reflection
of choices poorly made.

She manipulates,
a child in disguise,
passing off her struggles
as everyone's responsibility,
a game of blame
weary and worn.

Beneath the Family Tree

The Child in Her

Regressed to childish ways,
not from inability,
but from a willful refusal
to confront her own faults.

Her cries for help
are shadows of manipulation,
a tactic to make others
carry the burdens
she refuses to shoulder.

I see through her act,
a refusal to change,
to embrace accountability,
a cycle of deceit
that grows tiresome.

Conditional Affection

In my home,
love was measured in gifts and favors,
a system of control masked as generosity,
where affection came with a bill,
an expectation that weighed heavy.

Festivities should be light,
filled with joy and warmth,
but for me, they were a reminder
of the imbalance,
of love earned and not given,
of needs overshadowed by demands.

The gifts were not symbols of care,
but markers of obligation,
a power struggle disguised
in festive wrappings,
where true generosity was a ghost,
and love, a conditional currency.

Beneath the Family Tree

The Unseen Tax

To the world,
a child of privilege,
spoiled, entitled—
but they don't see the tax,
the hidden cost of each gift,
the price of every favor.

Possessions became a ledger,
where love was not given freely
but earned,
where joy was tainted
by the obligation to repay,
a debt never paid in full.

Guilt became the currency,
as needs were pushed aside
for a father's tantrum
or a mother's list of grievances,
each item a chain,
each request a weight.

Beneath the Family Tree

In the Shadow of Deception

Beneath the weight of so-called love,
I uncover the truth—
a shadow of expectation, not affection.

They preached duty as if sacred,
wrapping me in the chains of their promises,
threads of deceit woven into their commands.

Now I see their eyes,
quick to dismiss,
their silence crushing my voice,
my worth reduced to a whisper.

Anger rises, a smoldering ember,
betrayal I learned to endure,
only to find it was never mine to control,
but theirs to wield.

Grief settles in,
a constant companion,
reminding me of the roles I was forced to play,
shaped by their demands,
my true self lost in their shadows.

I was taught to bow,
to serve with a heart burdened by obligation,
my resentment masked,

Beneath the Family Tree

my spirit suppressed.

In the silence of their influence,
I reclaim what was mine,
a self unmarked by their cruelty,
a truth *finally freed* from their grip.

To My Younger Self

These poems are letters to the past, filled with reflection, advice, and healing messages directed to my younger self. This section speaks to the innocence lost and offers the guidance, wisdom, and care I wish I had received. It is a conversation with the child I was, extending the compassion and strength that time has granted.

To My Younger Self

Unwavering Support

Dear Younger Me,

I want you to know that I'm here for you,
To support your choices and stand by your side.
I won't hold you back or do things for you,
You must take the reins, and I'll guide you with pride.

You have the right to express yourself freely,
And pursue your path with courage and grace.
I'll never belittle or diminish your actions,
Your decisions are yours, and I'll embrace.

Unlike the family who failed to understand,
Who used you to feed their own needs and pride,
I will not infantilize or belittle your strength,
I'll support you through each step, no matter the tide.

Your mother's need to feel needed was her own,
Your father's judgment was his way to control.
And your sister's anger was her way of coping,
All their actions stemmed from wounds in their soul.

But here's my promise, clear and direct:
You're loved and supported, no matter the strain.
Be your own person, and trust in your power,
I'm with you each moment, through joy and through pain.

To My Younger Self

Trust Your Truth

Dear Younger Me, let me share a vital truth,
No matter who speaks—adult, friend, or foe—
Their words are not gospel, nor must you accept,
What they say as fact or let it shape your view.

Understand projection for what it is,
Their fears and flaws cast onto your heart.
What others claim does not define your worth,
Nor should it dictate the path you must chart.

Trust your instincts when doubts start to rise,
If something feels wrong, it likely is.
You're allowed to question, to push back with strength,
And declare with confidence, "This is not true."

Your truth is your own, no one else can claim,
Hold fast to your beliefs, and honor your gut.
You have the power to set your own course,
To respond with clarity and live with purpose.

To My Younger Self

Being True to Yourself

Dear Younger Me, it's okay if they don't like you,
Their rejection is a reflection of their fears.
True authenticity is rare and often daunting,
People who are secure will celebrate your truth.

Don't hide away your colors to fit in,
Stand proud in your authenticity and light.
The ones who resonate with your true self,
Will find you and cherish you just as you are.

To My Younger Self

The Power of Saying No

Dear Younger Me, it's okay to say no,
You have the right to set boundaries strong.
When overwhelmed, step back and breathe,
Your self-care is vital, your needs come first.

Don't be afraid to distance yourself from the strain,
Your well-being is your priority and right.
Remember, saying no is not weakness, but strength,
And your space is yours to protect and cherish.

To My Younger Self

Embracing Your Uniqueness

Dear Younger Me, you're unique and rare,
A sensitive soul with a light that shines.
Embrace your differences; let them be your guide,
Your sensitivity is a gift, not a curse.

Feel the energy around you and reject what isn't yours,
Your intuition is a strength, not a flaw.
You are meant to stand out and be true,
Celebrate who you are with pride and joy.

To My Younger Self

Don't chase the approval
of those who don't see you.
You don't owe them your shape,
your voice, or your choices.

Be yourself,
even when it feels like standing alone—
better to stand alone
than with a crowd that bends you
into something you're not.

Say no.
You can say it softly,
but say it with certainty.
Your time is precious,
and so are you.

To My Younger Self

Quiet In Crowds

Oh, little one, lost in a world too loud,
I wish I could tell you—
That your silence is not weakness,
That being overwhelmed is not your fault.

They called you shy, a label
You wore like a heavy cloak,
But inside, there was more—
A heart burdened by the clamor of too many voices,
Too many faces, too much confusion,
Unprepared to find your own voice.

No one gave you the tools
To understand your quiet strength,
Or to embrace your unique light
In a world that castrates the peculiar.

You were wrapped in the cocoon
Of an insecure mother's fears,
Misguided and misunderstood,
Not celebrated for the person you were becoming.

But now, from this place of knowing,
I want to tell you—
There is nothing wrong with you.
Your introversion, your authenticity,
Is a gift, not a flaw.

To My Younger Self

I see the beauty in your being,
The depth in your reserved grace,
And I cherish that inner child,
Telling you that it's all okay,
That you were always enough.

To My Younger Self

Walking Away

Sometimes,
they won't listen to you,
no matter how much you try.

And that's when it's okay
to walk away.

Their frustration isn't yours to carry,
and their anger
doesn't mean you're doing something wrong.

You are learning,
and that's what matters.
If they can't understand that,
you don't have to stay.

To My Younger Self

It's Okay to Be Different

You learn differently,
and that's not wrong.
It's just the way you're made.

When they talk,
and it doesn't make sense,
it's not your fault.
It's just the words they use,
not the way you see the world.

Keep asking,
keep picturing.
You'll find your way through,
even if they don't see it yet.

To My Younger Self

Speak Up

When they're rude,
when they make you feel like you're a problem,
I want you to speak up.
Tell them it's not fair.

It's not fair for them
to expect you to understand everything,
or to be perfect.

If they get upset,
you don't have to stay quiet.
Tell them you're learning,
and it's okay
if you need to ask for help.

To My Younger Self

Learning Is Messy

You're still learning.
Don't let them make you feel
like you're supposed to know everything.
It's okay to make mistakes—
that's how you figure it out.

You might feel small,
when they sigh or roll their eyes.
But don't let that stop you.
You are allowed to be wrong.
You are allowed to learn
in your own way.

To My Younger Self

Questions Are Allowed

They might get mad,
when you ask for the tenth time.
But I want you to know,
it's okay.

You're a kid.
How else are you supposed to learn
if you don't ask?
Their frustration isn't your fault.
You are allowed to ask questions.
You're allowed to say,
"I don't understand."

And if they snap at you,
it's not because of you.
They just don't know
how to help you yet.

To My Younger Self

The Way You Learn

You don't have to get it all at once.
The way you learn,
it's different,
and that's okay.

When they tell you things
that don't make sense,
it's not because you aren't listening.
It's just how you see the world,
through pictures,
through moments in your mind.

So next time,
try to see it—
the shovel, the shed.
And if it's not clear,
ask.
It's okay to ask,
you're still learning.

To My Younger Self

The Heart's Path

Ignore the clamor of disapproval,
the weight of others' expectations,
and take decisive steps forward.

The path you tread is yours alone,
unmarked by the fear of criticism
or the shadows of self-doubt.

Let your heart guide you,
its beat a compass in the flow
of your journey, unafraid to display
its raw, unfiltered truth.

As you press on, steady and unwavering,
trust in the gradual steps,
the routine that carries you forward,
knowing that perseverance will lead
to the horizon of your dreams.

To My Younger Self

The Flow of Determination

Decide and move forward,
let not the walls of criticism
or the echoes of self-doubt
halt your progress.

In the current of your aspirations,
let intuition steer the course,
unfettered by the weight of shame
or the clamor of dissenting voices.

Embrace your feelings,
let them guide you with authenticity,
wear your heart on your sleeve
as you navigate through the waves.

Continue with patience,
steady in your routines,
knowing that gradual progress
is the path to eventual success.

To My Younger Self

The Space Within

In the center of chaos,
there is a quiet space,
an inner haven where calm resides.

We guide through choices,
simple acts of drawing or listening,
each a thread leading
toward tranquility.

Breathing becomes the compass,
a rhythm to steer through turmoil,
as feelings are met with recognition,
honored in their presence.

In this space, the problem is seen
not as an obstacle, but a call
to find solutions,
to navigate the storm
with gentle steps and mindful calm.

To My Younger Self

The Breath of Calm

When emotions surge like waves,
we find solace in the breath,
a simple tool to steady the storm.

Inhale deeply, a slow rise
of the chest, filling the spaces
with air and tranquility,
exhale the tension, a release
of the turbulent currents within.

We offer choices, small anchors:
the feel of a pen against paper,
the soft strains of music,
each a lifeline to calm,
a gentle nudge toward inner peace.

In this moment, feelings are recognized,
each one valid, acknowledged
in their full weight, as breathing
and choice weave a tapestry
of calm amidst the tempest.

To My Younger Self

The Calming Space

In the storm of emotions,
a quiet room stands, an anchor
to which we can cling.

The space is a refuge,
its walls whispering promises
of peace and stillness,
a place to retreat when the world
becomes too loud, too overwhelming.

Here, we offer choices
like keys to unlock calm:
a blank page for drawing,
a melody to soothe the chaos,
each option a pathway
to serenity.

In this sanctuary,
breathing becomes a guide,
a rhythm to restore balance,
acknowledging the tumult within
while gently guiding it back to stillness.

To My Younger Self

No to Impressing

Don't waste your coins
on clothes for others,
on status symbols
that melt in the rain.

You do not need to impress
those you don't even like.
The right ones will see you
without the mask,
without the shine.

Love what you love,
stand in that truth.
Those who matter
will stay.

To My Younger Self

Your Own Path

They say,
"Do what makes sense."
But that sense belongs to them,
not you.

Your heart speaks
in a different language—
one that chases art,
words,
and freedom
in ways they'll never understand.

Follow it,
even when it scares you,
even when the road seems
lonely.

That's where you belong.

To My Younger Self

Trust Your Gut

Not every elder is wise.
Age doesn't bring clarity
to those who stay asleep.

You are not wrong
for doubting,
for questioning what they say
when it doesn't feel true.
Your gut will lead you
where they can't.
Follow it.

To My Younger Self

Your Worth Beyond Approval

When you're trying your best,
listening carefully,
following instructions,
and it still feels like you're falling short—

Understand this:
It's not you.
It's not your worth
that's at fault.

Sometimes,
when others project their own insecurities,
they make you feel insignificant
when all you're doing is trying to please.

You don't need approval
to know you're valuable.
Your worth isn't tied to how others see you
or whether they're pleased.

Mistakes are not failures.
They're opportunities to learn,
to grow,
to become better.
Everyone makes mistakes—
it's a natural part of life.

To My Younger Self

Look at how you handle your own mistakes,
how you learn from them.
I want you to see
that this is how you build self-worth.

You are unique.
Your strengths are yours alone.
Embrace who you are,
without needing validation from others.

Your value is not measured
by the approval you receive,
but by your own recognition
of your worth,
your efforts,
and your growth.

To My Younger Self

Trust Yourself

Adults don't always have the answers.

Those who guide you don't know more than you.
Neither do those who raise you.
Even I don't know what's right for you.

Trust yourself,
even when others say otherwise.
Remember, teachers can be wrong,
adults can be wrong,
but they rarely admit it.
A good person admits
when they're wrong,
but admitting mistakes
can be uncomfortable.

You've inherited habits
that aren't honest.
Behaviors passed down
that weren't true or kind.
I'm working on being better,
on admitting my own mistakes,
and I hope those who guide you are, too.

The actions you see—
the lack of honesty,
the disregard for your feelings—

To My Younger Self

are toxic.
Your feelings are important,
and you deserve to be yourself,
without shame or fear.

There's nothing wrong with you.
There's nothing wrong with how you feel.
Even if others don't see it,
you are valid.
You are allowed to trust yourself
and your own understanding.

To My Younger Self

Room To Breathe

Make room to breathe,
A quiet place just for you,
To craft and dream without the fear,
Without the harsh critique you hear.
A gentle space to show your truth,
To bare your heart and free your youth.

A solitude to calm the tide,
To let the surging waves subside,
Energy to softly mend,
To know the peace of self, my friend.
Step by step, and day by day,
As long as you keep finding your way.

To My Younger Self

Step by Step

Little by little,
you take a step forward.
There's no need to rush,
just move at your own pace.
It's not about being perfect
or doing it all at once—
it's about making strides,
even if they're small.

What you need is space,
space to try
without the pressure of expectation,
to grow
without anyone measuring
each step.

To My Younger Self

Sanctuary for the Soul

You need space to be yourself,
to create without fear,
without eyes watching,
waiting for you to stumble.
You need room to breathe,
free from judgment
or the weight of criticism
pressing down on you.

You need a place where you can be vulnerable,
where expressing yourself
isn't met with hesitation
or second guesses.
You just need the quiet
to hear your own thoughts,
to feel your own feelings,
without anyone else's
pushing in.

To My Younger Self

Lessons for a Younger Self

The world will be harsh,
doubt and fear will shadow you,
judgment may weigh heavy.

Not everyone will see your worth,
but their view does not define you.

Embrace your vulnerabilities;
they are the heart of who you are.
Stumble, falter—imperfection is your ally.

Amid the noise, trust yourself.
Your value lies within,
not in others' eyes.

Face the trials with courage,
hold fast to your inner strength.
This is the truth I wish you knew.

Becoming

Capturing the journey of self-discovery, growth, and resilience. These poems chart the course from darkness to light, illustrating moments of despair alongside glimpses of hope and clarity. This section explores the process of healing, acknowledging past wounds while celebrating the power of transformation.

Becoming

Breaking the Cycle

Healing from her abuse
isn't simple,
it's layered with pain,
complicated by years of control
I didn't see for what it was.

I had to start by acknowledging
the truth—
that what I lived through
was manipulation,
not love.

Learning about covert narcissism
was the first step.
It opened my eyes
to the patterns,
the lies,
and most importantly,
it reminded me that none of it
was my fault.

I carry anger,
betrayal,
a deep ache that sits inside me.
But I know I can't suppress it,
can't push it down—
to heal,

Becoming

I have to feel it all.

Setting boundaries
has become my lifeline.
Clear and firm,
they protect me from her reach.
I've limited contact,
and when those boundaries are crossed,
there are consequences—
there have to be.

Physical distance,
emotional space—
I need both
to break the cycle,
to free myself
from the constant triggers
that surround her.

And it's not just her.
The family, too,
caught in her web,
either enablers or blind
to what she's done.
Support isn't something
I can find in them,
and that hurts,
but I've come to accept it.

Becoming

This journey is mine,
and while it's painful,
it's the only way
to reclaim myself,
to finally be free.

The Darkness We Name

Admitting it
Is letting the darkness rise,
Letting the buried wounds breathe.
It is not a cry for pity
Or a plea for understanding,
It is simply
Naming what has always been.

We speak the unspoken,
We peel back the layers,
We look,
We see.

Steps Toward Healing

Mindfulness keeps me grounded,
pulling me back
from the edge of my thoughts
when anxiety creeps in.
Breathing slowly,
I find my center again.
It's a small step,
but it matters.

Meditation helps, too.
A moment of stillness
in the chaos of my mind.
The weight of stress lifts,
if only for a while,
and I feel lighter,
a little more in control.

Journaling is where I pour it all out—
the pain, the confusion,
the things I can't say out loud.
It's my outlet,
a way to make sense
of what's inside,
to process,
to understand.

This journey isn't easy.

Becoming

It's long, it's hard,
but these steps I take—
they're necessary.
They help me reclaim myself,
piece by piece,
bit by bit.

Creating distance from my family,
that's the hardest part.
It feels like cutting ties
with the only life I've known.
But I know it's needed.
I can't heal
in the same space
that broke me.

So, I take the steps,
one by one.
Even when it hurts,
I know this is the way
to reclaim my sense of self,
to find peace
on my own terms.

Becoming

The Weight of Acceptance

I cannot change the past,
I cannot bend it to my will.
It happened.
This is where acceptance lives—
In the space between wishing
And knowing.

Acceptance does not mean peace,
It means standing firm,
No longer erasing the edges
Of the things that hurt.
It's recognizing the scars
And learning not to flinch.

Becoming

Reflection

The truth sits heavy in silence,
It waits to be called by name.
Admitting means unraveling,
Seeing what you've hidden,
The parts of the story
That make your skin crawl.
This is where the work begins—
No more excuses, no more blame,
Just the rawness of it all,
A mirror you can't turn away from.

Becoming

The Shifting Sands

Strength lies in resourcefulness,
reliability anchors me steadfast,
adaptability flows like shifting sands,
a leader steering through ever-changing tides.

Yet, in this vast expanse,
the terrain of boundaries is uneven.
My strengths are clear, my faults emerge,
clarity once came through dialogue and limits set.

Now, I embrace both strength and frailty,
honoring the space between deadlines and self-care.
In understanding my own limits,
I uncover the true measure of my strength.

The Undercurrent

Beneath the surface of my strengths,
A current of tension flows,
Resourceful and reliable,
Yet the weight of unspoken limits pulls.

I manage tasks with practiced grace,
Multitasking through the whirl of demands,
Pride in my ability to communicate,
To meet deadlines with precision.

Still, there lies a quiet struggle,
Setting boundaries, accepting fragility,
In the past, conversations have steadied my course,
A reminder that strength also means knowing when to ask for help.

Becoming

Finding acceptance in truth

To be loved
is to be seen
as you are,
to have your truth honored,
your essence celebrated,
no masks, no lies.

To be unloved
by the ones who gave you life—
there is no deeper wound,
no sharper ache.
I ache to find acceptance,
to be known, to be held
for all that I am.

And I wish this, too,
for every soul that doubts,
for those who feel unworthy
when they dare to reveal
the rawness of their being.

Becoming

The Constant Urge

There is a weight in my chest,
a relentless drive
that insists I must always be moving,
always be achieving.
Without this,
I feel diminished,
my value in question,
my worth uncertain.

Yet, I know that I must release,
let go of this incessant need
to constantly be productive.
There is a greater force at play,
guiding me towards freedom,
towards a future I can almost touch,
a home in the woods
where solitude awaits.

In the midst of this relentless push,
I must find moments to pause,
to recognize the present
and savor the time I have,
for soon I will be alone,
living in the space I've dreamt of,
a world of trees and silence.

Becoming

The Future and the Present

The distant sound of wood being cut
is a promise,
a reminder of what's to come.
The new home
on my secluded land
is taking shape,
its frame rising
with the potential of solitude.

Yet here, in the now,
I am trapped in the cycle
of ceaseless activity.
My mind is restless,
constantly pushing me
towards goals and actions,
while I struggle to enjoy
the present moments
with my family.

Everything is aligning
in ways unseen,
guiding me toward the life
I've envisioned.
I must learn to balance
the anticipation of what's coming
with the necessity of living
fully in the present.

Becoming

The Paradox of Progress

There is a paradox
in the pursuit of progress—
the need to be constantly moving
versus the call to let things unfold
in their own time.
I feel the pressure
to achieve, to act,
as if my worth is tied
to my productivity.

Yet, the truth is
that the universe has its own rhythm,
and I am not alone
in this journey.
The hands guiding me
are gentle, patient,
and the promise of independence
is growing ever closer.

Amidst the urgency,
there is a call for stillness,
to embrace the present,
to enjoy these fleeting moments
before I step into my new life.
The woods will soon be my sanctuary,
but for now, I must learn to cherish
the here and now.

Becoming

The Heavy Burden

When,
that's the question
that haunts me,
as I navigate this life
with its relentless obstacles.

I've toiled,
putting in the hours,
but now,
my motivation wanes,
sapped by the struggle
to achieve goals
that feel ever elusive.

I found a glimmer of joy
in my work,
yet even that
is overshadowed
by the toxic environment
I am forced to endure.

The question lingers—
have I done enough?
It's a measure of inadequacy,
a reminder that the escape
I yearn for
seems as distant as ever.

Becoming

This place,
with its suffocating presence,
is a prison
that stifles my spirit.
My dreams of freedom
and personal space
are obscured by the harsh realities
of financial strain and personal control.

The world outside
seems indifferent,
a place where kindness
and compassion are rare.
I seek peace,
a sanctuary from the cruelty
and the narcissistic behaviors
that have eroded my hope.

In this struggle,
I am weary,
drained by the constant battle
to move forward
in a world that feels
both harsh and unforgiving.

Becoming

From Wonder to Woe

Childhood was a realm
of wonder,
where each day
held the promise of joy,
and the future
was a canvas of potential.

You lived in the present,
where every moment
was new,
and the world
was small and manageable.

But then adulthood
unfolded its dark truths,
revealing a landscape
marred by disappointment,
cruelty, and unfulfilled dreams.

The excitement of youth
gave way to the harsh
realities of life,
the beauty of hope
replaced by the grind
of daily struggles.

Your dreams,

Becoming

once vibrant and alive,
became shattered,
lost in the shadows
of a disillusioned reality.

You seek solace
in the things
that help you escape,
but the hope
you once cherished
is now a distant memory,
fading into the darkness.

Becoming

The Fall from Innocence

As a child,
hope was a constant companion,
a light that guided each day.
You embraced the world
with wide eyes,
unaware of the shadows
lurking in the corners.

The future was a land
of endless possibilities,
where dreams were vivid
and every moment
was a new adventure.

Then, adulthood arrived,
and with it,
a harsh reality.
The brightness of youth
diminished,
replaced by the weight
of responsibilities and suffering.

The innocence you held
was shattered,
leaving behind
a landscape of broken dreams
and fading memories.

Becoming

Now,
you see the world's ugliness
clearly,
the cruelty and darkness
that were once hidden.
You cling to fleeting escapes,
your hope dwindling,
your dreams in fragments.

In the mirror,
you search for answers,
for someone to blame,
but is it you
or the world
that failed to meet
your youthful expectations?

Becoming

The Loss of Youthful Hope

Childhood was a time
of pure excitement,
where every day
was a new beginning,
and the future
held endless promise.

You embraced life
with wide-eyed wonder,
unaware of the suffering
and responsibilities
that lay ahead.

Adulthood brought
a harsh reality,
a world marred by
cruelty and shattered dreams.

The joy of youth
was replaced by the weight
of disillusionment,
as the bright future
you envisioned
became a distant memory.

Now, you seek solace
in fleeting escapes,

Becoming

your dreams in tatters,
your hope diminishing.

You wonder,
as you face your reflection,
whether the fault lies
within yourself
or in the world
that failed to deliver
on the promises of your youth.

Becoming

Lost Dreams

I try to recall
the dreams of my youth,
the vision of adulthood
that seemed so clear,
so attainable.

I imagined a life
of creation,
of artistic pursuits,
of freedom from control.

Now, I face a different reality,
one marked by financial strain,
by the struggle to find
a stable path.

The dreams of a creative career,
of independence,
seem distant,
clouded by the challenges
of adulthood.

I grapple with regret,
with the sense
that time has passed
without the fulfillment
I once envisioned.

Becoming

A Fresh Start

The old me is dead,
buried in the past.
I've let go of the life
that no longer serves me,
but now I'm waiting
for something new
to begin.

I'm ready for a fresh start,
ready to live my own life,
but the waiting
is killing me.

I don't know how much longer
I can hold on,
but I'm trying.
I'm trying to believe
that something better
is coming.

Becoming

The Solitude of Creation

Creation is a sanctuary,
a realm where numbness fades,
where the act of making
brings solace.

In the waiting,
the uncertainty,
there is a lesson,
a call to trust
the unfolding process.

Amidst the haze of burnout,
the exhaustion of endless effort,
find comfort in small victories,
in the act of persistently creating,
of continuing despite
the void of immediate reward.

Balance emerges in the solitude,
in the focus on joy,
in the slow and steady march
toward the liberation
that lies beyond the familiar confines.

Becoming

The Path of Persistence

Slow and steady,
a mantra for the weary,
a promise in the fog
of indecision.

In the stillness of each step,
the journey unfolds,
slowly,
persistently,
with no sudden leaps
or abrupt changes.

Align with joy,
trust in the gentle flow,
the rhythm of gradual progress
amidst the noise of self-doubt.

Even in moments of exhaustion,
when the path seems endless,
continue, unhurried,
for success is a steady
revelation,
not an instant triumph.

Becoming

The Freedom in Fragility

Embrace vulnerability,
the rawness of the open heart,
for in its exposure
lies the key to true freedom.

Yet, the environment,
a cauldron of toxic interactions,
brews confusion and apathy,
numbing the spirit
with its relentless strain.

Burnout is not merely fatigue
but a hollow echo
of an existence
seeking respite
from ceaseless discord.

To escape is to live,
to seek independence
beyond the smothering grasp
of familial manipulation,
beyond the weight
of unmet expectations.

BECOMING

The Unwavering Course

Act now, dismissing the noise
of external judgments and internal fears.

Decide with conviction,
navigate through the currents
of your own intuition,
and let not the voices of doubt
or the specter of failure deter you.

Embrace your journey with openness,
allowing feelings to surface,
each step a testament to your resolve
to follow through, no matter how gradual.

Even in moments of exhaustion,
when the urge to give up beckons,
continue with the rhythm of persistence,
for each day brings you closer
to the success you seek.

The Waiting Game

I'm stuck in this waiting game—
for money,
for freedom,
for the chance
to finally leave.

Maybe I'll win the lottery,
maybe my business
will finally take off,
or maybe I'll inherit
everything when they're gone.

I don't know.
I just need something,
anything,
to pull me out of this hell.
I can't live like this
anymore.

Becoming

Little by Little

It's not about doing it all
in one giant leap.
It's about moving forward,
even when the steps are small.

Little by little,
I find my way,
as long as I have space—
space to try,
space to fail
and still know
I'm making progress.

Each step counts,
each moment of quiet
helps me grow.

Becoming

Boundaries I Cannot Speak

I am always afraid
To draw the line,
As if by saying "no,"
I'm erasing
A part of myself.

But boundaries are not prisons—
They are the walls
I need
To stand tall
In my own space.

I am learning
That to say "no"
Is to say "yes"
To the self I've always hidden.

The Vision

I have a vision
of living the life I want,
of independence and space,
of freedom from the constraints
that bind me here.

Pride in the journey,
in the lessons learned,
in the healing accomplished,
in the boundaries set,
yet impatience gnaws,
a hunger for now,
for the life I dream.

Life is fleeting,
a canvas of fleeting moments,
and I seek to paint it
with fulfillment and service,
to explore spirituality and magic,
to empower, to be,
to fully embrace the person
I am becoming.

Becoming

The Quest for True Freedom

The sadness of a life
lived just for survival,
without spark, without joy,
without the freedom to dance
in my own space,
to be, to act,
without judgment or fear.

I don't want to be one of the trapped,
living a life of resignation,
of stuck in the cycle,
of working just to make ends meet,
without ever reaching for more.
I seek the freedom to choose,
to create, to live.

Becoming

The Point of Departure

What is the point?
It's the sense of being trapped,
a small town offering nothing
but a chance to save and scheme,
a waiting room for freedom.

Fear whispers of expenses,
rent and groceries,
the daily grind of a 9-to-5,
and the labor of building a dream,
a business in the dark.

But maybe this is the path,
the opportunity hidden in the struggle,
a chance to align with my true self,
to write and create,
to embrace the magic within.

Maybe the unhappiness is a signal,
a call to act,
to live fully and authentically,
to find joy in service,
in helping others,
in discovering what truly lights me up.

Finding Home

Dedicated to reclaiming identity and embracing uniqueness. These poems celebrate defiance, the breaking away from family expectations, and the quest to find a sense of belonging. They reflect on unraveling ties that once bound me and piecing together a new understanding of home, rooted in self-acceptance rather than family ties.

Creating Without Fear

What I need is space—
to create without the weight
of judgment on my shoulders.
To express myself freely,
without fear
of being picked apart.

In the quiet,
I can let the walls down,
let myself be vulnerable.
That's where the best of me lives—
not in perfection,
but in the raw, unfiltered moments
that no one else sees.

Solitude

Solitude,
that's where I find balance.
A quiet room,
a moment alone
to feel grounded
in my own skin again.

I can't think straight
when there's noise all around.
I need that stillness
to regulate my energy,
to calm the chaos
that stirs when too many voices
press in on me.

Give me space,
and I'll find my way
back to myself.

Boundaries Like Shields

Boundaries—
I set them now,
though you see them as walls.
They are shields,
built from years of knowing
that every step closer
is a step back into her game.

You ask why I keep away.
I ask why you never saw
the chains she used
to keep me close.

Finding Home

The Space I Need

Distance,
not just miles,
but between hearts that could never meet.
The space I carve is for survival.
They call it rebellion,
I call it freedom.

I must step back,
or be swallowed again,
into her web of subtle cruelty,
where I am always the one to blame.

Finding Home

The Essentials

Today, I gathered the pieces of myself,
each one a fallen leaf
in the forest of my mind.
No need for grand rituals,
no feast of perfection.
Just the soft hum of the earth
beneath my feet,
whispering its ancient truths.

I didn't chase the sun,
but let it find me,
its warmth seeping through the cracks
I hadn't noticed.
Each step I took
was a breath,
a pulse of life
in a world that asked nothing of me.

The air tasted clean,
as if it had never known the weight
of voices,
and the sky—
so clear it could have been
a memory of stillness—
wrapped me in silence.

There, in the quiet dance

Finding Home

of wind and light,
I became whole again,
unburdened by the noise
of what the world thinks I need.
Just the roots of solitude,
the bloom of fresh air,
and the quiet
growing steady inside me.

Finding Home

Clearing the Noise

It was quiet today,
and that made all the difference.
I didn't wake up to chaos,
didn't have to carry anyone else's weight.

The air felt clean,
the sky didn't have
the usual haze.
For once, I could see clearly.

A walk in the forest,
time to clear out everything
that doesn't belong.
I felt lighter,
more grounded.
This is what I need—
solitude and fresh air.

Finding Home

A Good Day

I had a good day today.
Not because of anything special—
but because I was alone.

No one to overwhelm me,
no voices or tension
dragging me down.

I could just be.
Got some sun,
took a walk in the trees,
and let everything else fall away.

It's amazing how much better I feel
when I don't have to deal
with anyone else.

Finding Home

Centered

Today, I didn't feel the usual pull—
that tension in my chest,
the anxious feeling that makes it hard
to stay grounded.

I had space.
Woke up to quiet,
no one to manage,
no one to take from me.

I could focus,
feel centered,
breathe deeply.

This is what I need—
to be alone,
to step outside,
to clear my head
and feel connected to myself again.

No stress,
no worry,
just space to be.

Fresh Air

I stepped outside,
into air that felt real—
no weight,
no heaviness
from the world above.

It was just me,
the sun,
the forest.
I could clear my head
with every breath,
every step.

No one else around
to cloud my thoughts,
no voices
to pull me in every direction.

It's so simple.
Just me,
the air,
and the sky.

Simple Truth

It's obvious what the issue is.
I'm happier today,
lighter,
not dragged down by the weight
of triggered emotions
or the stress
that usually clings to me.

I didn't eat much differently,
but today wasn't about food.
It was the solitude—
waking up to my own space,
no one around,
no noise.

I could breathe,
I could center,
I could be still.

Forest bathing,
sunlight,
exercise.
It all worked.
Fresh air and no one else's energy
to overwhelm me.

It's simple, really.

Finding Home

This is what I need:
solitude,
fresh air,
movement.
And then, maybe,
a little balance in what I eat.

Finding Home

The Journey of Freedom

Freedom is a distant shore,
a horizon reached through
slow, deliberate strides
against the tide of expectation.

In the pursuit of independence,
each step, each decision
is a rebellion against
the chains of toxic environments,
against the weight of familial manipulation.

There is no rush,
only the steady rhythm
of progress,
of saving, creating,
waiting for the right moment.

Until then, navigate
the path of least resistance,
guided by intuition,
embracing each moment
as a chance to reclaim
a piece of the self.

Finding Home

The Room to Be

All I need is space—
to be,
to breathe,
to feel without someone
telling me I'm wrong.

I need a place where I can create,
where my thoughts can flow
without someone else's words
blocking the way.
A space to be vulnerable,
to let myself feel
without fear of being judged.

It's simple, really—
I just need the room
to be myself.

People Pleaser

I spent years
being a people pleaser,
building relationships
on the back of my own pain.
I gave too much,
sacrificed too much,
just to make others happy.

But I'm done with that.
I've let go of those friendships,
let go of the life
that no longer serves me.
I'm ready for something new,
something real,
something that's mine.

Finding Home

Escaping the Cycle

There's a reason I run,
why I leave
before the arguments start,
before the drama takes root
and pulls me under.

They think I'm distant,
cold,
ungrateful for the ties
we share.
But I know the truth—
distance is survival
when the ones who raised you
are drowning in their own poison.

Happiness in Distance

I am lighter
when they aren't around,
when the air isn't thick
with their judgment
or the tension
they refuse to see.

My happiness
comes in the spaces
where they do not exist,
where their voices
can't reach me.

And in those moments,
I remember
what it feels like
to breathe.

Finding Home

Embracing the Silence

There is peace
in the quiet,
far from their noise.

Their voices echo
in an empty room,
and I am grateful
not to be there,
not to be the one
they swallow whole.

They don't see the absence,
they only feel the silence
and call it everyone else's fault.

Breaking Free

It was only when I moved away
that I learned to see
Holidays and festivities
as they were meant to be,
free of strings,
free of control.

The real gift was freedom,
the real joy,
in celebrating without the weight
of obligation,
without the specter of guilt
tugging at every festivity.

Even now, receiving gifts
feels like a burden,
an echo of a past
where generosity was a trap,
and love was something
that had to be earned.

Quiet Rebellion

I gather quietly,
Slip away,
Rearrange my day
To avoid the clash
Of their presence.

It's a quiet rebellion—
Not to fight,
Not to engage,
But to find my own way
Through the silence
They don't understand.

Finding Home

A Life in Fragments

I gather in fragments,
Bits of space,
Essentials carried
From shared rooms
Into the corners
Where I can breathe.

Each step away from them
Is a step toward freedom,
A space carved out
By the quiet act
Of avoidance.

Finding Home

Learning to Let Go

Plans bend,
Moments shift.
I've learned to let them go,
To fold into new shapes
When they fill the air.

It's a strange kind of freedom,
To adapt,
To move quietly through rooms
Where I do not linger.

Finding Home

Not Theirs to Shape

I thought my worth
Was theirs to define,
Their approval
The only currency
That mattered.

But I am learning—
Their gaze is not my mirror,
Their judgment
Not my truth.

Finding Home

Learning to Unfold

Healing is untangling
The knots of their expectations
From the threads of my being.

It is saying "no"
And feeling the tremor
Of fear pass,
But not break me.

It's understanding
That I'm not here
To be molded
By their hands.

The Unburied

To admit it
Is to unearth the pieces
You buried long ago.
It's not about the pain,
But the truth,
The unflinching clarity
Of what was real.

You bring it to the surface,
Hold it in your hands,
And let it rest,
For the first time,
Without shame.

Reclaiming Power

The past will knock,
But you don't have to answer.
You can open the door
And stand firm,
Knowing what you know now.

Forgiveness is the quiet power
Of saying,
"I see you,
But you are not my keeper."

Finding Home

In the Driver's Seat

To move on
Is to step into the driver's seat
Of your own life.
It's more than a destination,
It's the ability
To chart your own course,
To know where you'll go
And where you won't.

It's not about the absence of pain,
But the mastery of it—
Knowing it no longer
Has the final say.

Finding Home

Beyond the Edge

Moving on doesn't mean escape,
It means you can step
Without looking back
At what once chased you.

The past still lingers,
But you are no longer bound
By its grasp.
You've learned the shape of it,
And now you hold the reins.

A Shift

Acceptance isn't surrender—
It's the shift in perspective,
The quiet shift
From victim to survivor,
From trapped to free.

It's standing in the same storm
But knowing
You are not the same as before.

What Remains

Forgiveness is not forgetting.
It's carrying the weight differently,
So that it no longer crushes,
But simply rests,
A part of you,
But not the whole.

You still feel the tremors sometimes,
But the ground beneath your feet
No longer gives way.

Finding Home

Taking the Reins

The moment it stops being theirs,
The power shifts.
This is acceptance—
Realizing no one else
Will pull you from the fire.
It's your own hands
That steer this life,
And no one else can choose
What path you'll walk.

The grip loosens
As the weight is lifted,
Not from forgetting
But from holding yourself
Accountable.

Finding Home

Self-Reliance

I will not lay my burdens bare,
Seeking solace in another's gaze;
Sympathy's false comfort, I reject,
For I heal best within my own space.

Distance is my shield and guide,
In the quiet of my solitude,
I watch for the shadows in their cheers,
For any lack of true delight reveals deceit.

Friends who revel in my small defeats
Are no more than shadows in my path,
Their joy in my failures a mirror of their own,
A reflection of their need for my downfall.

I sever ties with those who limit,
Choosing not to be a pawn in their game;
In peace, success, and freedom, I find my strength,
Embracing the journey of my own making.

Finding Home

The Invisible Line

I am a vessel of resourcefulness,
A ship steering through deadlines,
Every task a wave, every project a port,
My compass always pointing to "completed."

Yet, the horizon holds a fog,
Boundaries blur, limits stretch,
The map of my strengths,
Unfolds with gaps where balance should be.

In the past, I've charted these waters,
Through honest dialogue, through adjustment,
Seeking not just to lead, but to find my own shore.

The Authentic Self

In the quest for self-improvement,
I realize the fun was never in the bottle,
But in the silent moments of clarity,
The gentle touch of genuine joy.

I will stop seeking approval,
Stop buying friendship with gestures,
If reciprocity is absent, I'll step back,
Reclaim my time and energy.

My journey now lies in balance,
In healthy choices and honest connections,
A life enriched not by excess,
But by purposeful, nurturing actions.

Finding Home

Boundaries in the Dark

I used to pour my nights away,
A six-pack, then another,
Hours slipping into the abyss,
Lost in the haze of false fun.

Now, I seek to draw a line,
A boundary where I used to drown,
No more runaway nights,
Just moments crafted by choice.

The echoes of laughter,
No longer a mask for my discontent,
I seek the genuine joy
Of activities not fueled by a bottle.

Finding Home

A Reminder

When frustration rises,
and the weight of my situation bears down,

I remind myself:

I am making moves,
stepping toward change,
shaping my life
with each action I take.

I am crafting the future
I envision,
creating the life
I choose,
with determination and purpose.

Writing as Healing

Writing is my sanctuary,
a place where healing unfolds,
where my voice finds its truth,
and self-expression becomes
a conduit for fulfillment.

The process is natural,
a gift that feels both innate and profound,
a talent that channels
what flows from within,
without imitation,
but from a deeper, original source.

To see my words received
is to witness the potential
for connection and impact,
where success and joy align,
and writing becomes
a path to both personal and shared growth.

Finding Home

Building My Own Space

In their absence,
I collect pieces
Of a life they don't touch.

A cup,
A chair,
A blanket to pull close
In the quiet of my own room.
I make this space
Out of things gathered
When no one was watching.

Finding Home

A Year from Now

A year from now,
these walls will not hold me,
the weight I carry today
will be lighter,
or gone.

I am shaping something new,
building with quiet hands,
each small step a stone laid
for the life I deserve.

What I see now as struggle,
will be the strength
I didn't know I was gathering.

In a year,
the faces that haunt me
will blur,
their voices will fade.
I'll stand taller,
with the space to breathe
that I carved for myself.

The days may feel long now,
but I am moving—
slow, steady,
toward the future I'm creating,

Finding Home

where peace and freedom wait
on the other side of today.

Finding Home

Reclaiming Freedom

It's time to leave behind
the world you once knew,
to step away from lives shaped by greed
and despair.

Prepare to discover,
to learn the skills of survival,
to build and create
with your own hands.
This is your purpose—
to find independence,
to reclaim your life
in a world that's yours.

Find a community
of like-minded souls.
Start doing things for yourself.
Say goodbye to the old ways
and enter a realm
free from tyranny.

Nature holds the answers.
Learn to forage,
to use natural remedies.
Understand the wild plants,
their healing gifts.
Become a steward of the land,

Finding Home

embracing ancient practices.

Understand the flow of energies,
the harmony with nature.
You are part of this world,
work with the elements,
to shape your own path.

Barter and trade,
never paying full price
for anything.
Everything in this world
is constructed,
and so are its prices.

All you seek
is peace and alignment,
a life where you are free,
a home in harmony
with the natural world.

Finding Home

Making Space Where They Aren't

I carve out space
Where they can't reach me,
Collecting moments
When the air is clear.

I've learned the art
Of moving unseen,
Of bending plans,
Of shaping silence
Into something
That feels like peace.

Finding Home

The Choice of Freedom

I face the choice each day:
To be bound by their shadows
Or to stand alone in my light.
Their power is a tradition I reject,
Their control a chain I break.

In the distance, I find my peace,
Away from the passive-aggressive whispers
That once stifled my voice.
Here, I forge my path to freedom,
Self-reliant, unshackled, whole.

No more will I seek their approval,
Nor will I play the part of their puppet.
I choose success, I choose peace,
And in the quiet of my own space,
I find the freedom to be myself.

About the Author

Drew Mackby Sand is a Canadian artist and writer whose literary journey began with his first publication while still in his teens. This early success ignited a lifelong passion for exploration in both his artistic and academic pursuits. Equipped with several art degrees and a diverse career across various creative fields, Drew has remained dedicated to his artistic passions. His writing and poetry, chosen as his primary means of deep self-expression, reflect his unique perspective as a self-described black sheep. Through his evocative and heartfelt poetry, Drew connects profoundly with readers, capturing the essence of his experiences and reflections. With a genuine and imaginative spirit, he invites readers to embark on a journey through the rich landscapes of his creative work.

www.ingramcontent.com/pod-product-compliance
Lightning Source LLC
Chambersburg PA
CBHW070542010526
44118CB00012B/1195